£5.99
AK
BA/c10D
26

SETTLE
AND
CARLISLE
MEMORIES

1. *Frontispiece* Class 9F 2-10-0 No 92156, in charge of a southbound
freight, climbs the 1 in 100 up to Ais Gill. The location is between
Birkett tunnel and Mallerstang, 28 January 1967. C. E. WESTON

SETTLE AND CARLISLE MEMORIES

ROGER SIVITER A.R.P.S.

Unicorn Books

ACKNOWLEDGEMENTS

I would like to thank the following people for their help in compiling this book: Neil Caplan, Dave Lacey, Christina Siviter, Joan Wappett, Patrick Whitehouse and Mick York; all the photographers who let me choose from their picture collections and, when necessary, let me make prints from their precious negatives; the railwaymen who run the Settle & Carlisle; and last but not least, the Friends of the Settle & Carlisle who, through their unstinting efforts over a not inconsiderable period of time, have been so instrumental in saving this wonderful railway line.

Other Titles by Roger Siviter

Tempo of Steam, Ian Allan
Steam Specials, David & Charles
Focus on South African Steam, David & Charles
Handbook of Railway Photography, David & Charles
The Settle to Carlisle, a Tribute, Baton Press
The Welsh Marches, Baton Transport
Scottish Steam Routes, Baton Transport
Diesels and Semaphores, OPC
Great Western Mainline Steam (Review of 1985), Kingfisher
Waverley, Portrait of a Famous Route, Kingfisher
BR Steam Surrender, Kingfisher
50s in Devon & Cornwall, Kingfisher
37s in the Highlands, Kingfisher
A Photographer's Guide to Railways, Peerage Books

Other Titles in the Unicorn Railway series

30 Years of Trainspotting by John Stretton
Cotswold Memories by Dennis Edwards and Ron Pigram
Great Central Rail Tour by John M C Healy
Leicestershire Railway Memories by John Stretton
Midland through the Peak by Brian Radford
Oxfordshire Railway Memories by John Stretton

First published in 1990 by
UNICORN BOOKS,
16 Laxton Gardens,
Paddock Wood,
Kent TN12 6BB

© Roger Siviter 1990

ISBN 185241 012 4

Typeset by Vitaset, Paddock Wood
Printed by Amadeus Press
Huddersfield, Yorks.

Jacket illustrations

Front Cover. 9F No 92004 approaches Ais Gill summit with a southbound goods, February 1967. PAUL RILEY

Back Cover *Top*. *Princess Elizabeth* in charge of a northbound special crosses Sheriff's Brow viaduct, 25 July 1987. JOHN KENWARD

Bottom. 9F No 92009 approaches Kirkby Stephen with a Long Meg-Widnes anhydrite train, 29 April 1967. LES NIXON

Contents

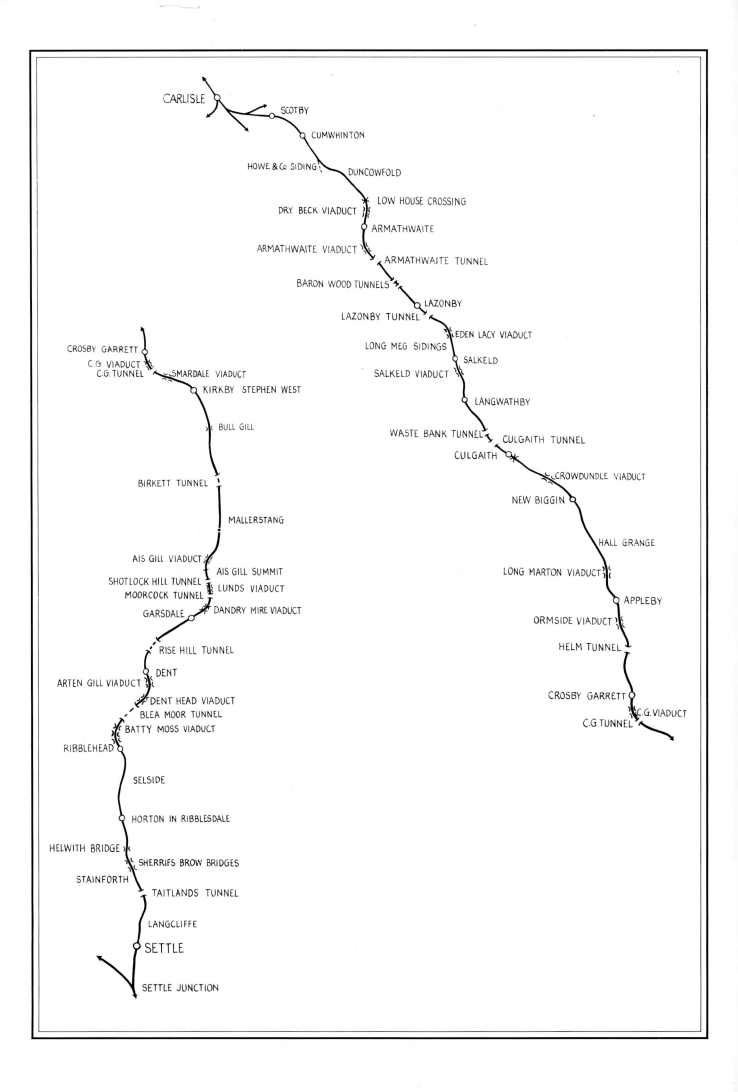

Historical Background:

The St.Pancras Route

It is a privilege to contribute these notes to a splendid new 'Portrait' of the Settle & Carlisle Line which now has such a tremendous following, including many people who are not railway enthusiasts as such but who have fallen under the spell of its scenery and engineering. With my own books in praise of the West Highland Line and the Waverley Line, I cannot rate the Settle & Carlisle Line as first among all *British* scenic routes, but I hold it to be the most dramatic and fascinating of all those in England.

I have been an ardent admirer of the Settle & Carlisle for over fifty years. This means that I knew the Line well when it still served an Anglo-Scottish trunk route. But memory needs to stretch back even further than this to see the St Pancras Route in operation as a worthy rival to the East and West Coast Routes. Yet, even in its heyday, the St Pancras Route did not attract the same intense interest of railway enthusiasts as the rival routes did. It is sharp irony that the Settle & Carlisle Line, which was built to complete the Route, has come to command such great interest and support only after the latter had been reduced to virtual insignificance – without even one through passenger train between the Thames and the Clyde!

The story of the Settle & Carlisle Line is dominated, of course, by the history of the Midland Railway Company. The Midland was a great company indeed in every important aspect of railway development and operation. However, until the mid-1860s, few observers thought it probable that the Midland would become responsible, with its Scottish partners, for a third Anglo-Scottish trunk route. It is true that by then the Midland was a powerful company with its firm base in the industrial heartland of Central England, but the axis of its system lay north-east to south-west – from York to Bristol. This pattern stemmed from the 'mixed bag' of small companies which amalgamated in 1844 to form the Midland Railway Company, the most enduring contribution to British railway development made by George Hudson.

In 1865 the outstanding weakness of the Midland Railway was its lack of a line of its own into London from its southern railhead at Bedford. For access to a London terminus, the Midland depended on the co-operation of other companies. Originally, the Midland had worked with the London & North Western Railway in spite of the growing rivalry between the two companies. But the capacity of the LNWR's line from Rugby to Euston was inadequate to handle so much

traffic and it was the Midland's trains which suffered the most frequent and serious delays from this congestion. This forced the Midland to turn, in 1862, to the Great Northern Railway, using the line to Kings Cross via the Bedford-Hitchin branch. Once again, the combined traffic became too great for line capacity. The Midland had no option but to build a line of its own from Bedford to London. The London Extension Line was completed on 1 October 1868 with the opening of St Pancras Station. This was one of the grand occasions in our railway history and vital for the future of the Midland Railway.

Away to the north-west, however, the Midland was a long way short of Carlisle where it would be able to link up with the Glasgow & South Western Railway's Nithsdale Line to Glasgow, and with the Waverley Line of the North British Railway to Edinburgh. The Midland's railhead was at Ingleton which had been reached as far back as 1850 from Clapham on the Skipton & Lancaster Line (popularly known as the Little North Western). This meant that the Midland could gain Carlisle only over the Lancaster & Carlisle Railway which formed part of the West Coast Route. Though the Lancaster & Carlisle was closely allied to the LNWR, it was willing to work also with the Midland and it agreed to build a branch line from Low Gill to Ingleton, via Sedbergh, and work began in 1857. There was a serious setback for the Midland before the branch was completed: in 1859 the LNWR took complete control of the Lancaster & Carlisle under the terms of their famous 999 Years Leasing Agreement. When the Low Gill-Ingleton line was opened in 1861, the Midland's access to Carlisle was at the mercy of its most inveterate rival.

The LNWR and the Caledonian Railway had no intention of helping the Midland and its Scottish allies to a share of Anglo-Scottish traffic over the West Coast Route. The Caledonian saw the arrival of the Midland at Carlisle as the one development which would ensure the independent existence of the Glasgow & South Western Railway, whose Nithsdale Line had been so under utilised since its completion in 1850. Also, the Caledonian wished to deprive its great rival, the North British Railway, of the promised through traffic over the Waverley Line. The LNWR allowed the Midland's trains to run only as far as Tebay, where it made life miserable for the Midland's passengers bound for Carlisle and Scotland. It was a stark choice which faced the Midland Railway: either to abandon its attempt to operate an effective service to Scotland, or to accept the challenge of building a new line from Settle to Carlisle. The challenge was huge because the LNWR held the Upper Lune Valley and the only feasible course would be to strike north towards the Eden Valley across many miles of mountainous terrain.

Wealthy as the Midland Railway had become, it was a courageous decision to undertake the construction of the 72 miles of line from Settle to Carlisle. Despite the fierce opposition of the LNWR and the Caledonian, the Authorisation Act was obtained in 1865. At this point, however, the Midland's board of directors wavered and delayed the work. This was, perhaps, understandable because the estimated cost per mile of the Settle & Carlisle Line had been put at £30,000 – an enormous sum in the 1860s. The Midland went so far as to introduce an Abandonment Bill, but this was vigorously opposed by other interested parties, notably by the Lancashire & Yorkshire Railway and the North British Railway. The Lancashire & Yorkshire knew that unless the Midland built the Line it could never share in the growing traffic between Liverpool, Manchester and Central Scotland. The L&Y had reached the Midland at Hellifield over its branch from Blackburn and it would thus be able to operate through carriages for Glasgow and Edinburgh. The North British Railway needed the Midland at Carlisle if its Waverley Line was not to be an expensive failure. Such resolute opposition secured the rejection of the Bill and work was started in 1869.

The dramatic story of the construction of the Settle & Carlisle Line has been told many times. All that need be noted here is that it proved an even tougher proposition than had been envisaged. Despite the succession of major viaducts and tunnels high up in the Pennines, the grading of the Line up to its summit of 1,169 feet at Ais Gill was severe. The actual cost came to £50,000 a mile – that is, the *money* cost, because the costs in time and sadly, in lives lost, proved exceptionally heavy (Terry Coleman's *The Railway Navvies* (1981) is recommended reading here). Although the work occupied some seven years, it was a magnificent engineering achievement to begin freight working over the Line in 1875, with a full passenger service in 1876.

Completion of the Settle & Carlisle Line was a triumph for the Midland Railway and its Scottish partners. The St Pancras Route confirmed the Midland as one of the top three British railway companies and it brought substantial benefits for the Glasgow & South Western and the North British. However, the route had come late in the day and the East and West Coast Routes were firmly established. The latter retained important advantages over the St Pancras Route, particularly in the matter of length of route. The St Pancras Route to Glasgow was 23 miles longer than the West Coast Route (25 miles when a call was made at Sheffield). The heavy grading of the climb to Ais Gill at least balanced the West Coast Route's climbs over Shap and Beattock, especially during the all too frequent harsh winter conditions along the Settle & Carlisle Line. The East Coast Route to Edinburgh was 13 miles less than via the St Pancras Route and it had the advantage of relatively easy grading throughout.

These considerations alone made it impracticable for the St Pancras Route to compete with its rivals if it ever came to all-out competition over journey times. This was underlined dramatically during the 1895 'Race to the North' between the East and West Coast Routes. But the St Pancras Route was largely shielded by the agreement between its rivals to maintain a *minimum journey time* of 8hrs 15mins between London and Scotland which held good until the 1930s. From the outset, therefore, the Midland and its Scottish allies based the appeal of their route on its far greater scenic interest and its very high standards of passenger comfort. Before the 1914 War there were many travellers who were not in such a hurry as to set great store by a saving of 30-40mins on their journeys to and from Scotland.

In any case, the commercial appeal of the St Pancras Route rested largely on the fact that it provided such a direct link between many important cities and industrial areas and with Central Scotland: Leicester, Nottingham, Derby, Sheffield and Leeds. It was essential therefore that even the principal Corridor Expresses should call at several of these cities. There never was an economic basis for really long nonstop runs over the St Pancras Route – like those achieved during the latter 1920s and 30s by the East and West Coast Routes. A particularly interesting sidelight is that the St Pancras Route to Glasgow had four sets only of water-troughs, including the Settle & Carlisle's troughs at Garsdale set at just above 1,000 feet (the highest troughs in the world).

Nevertheless, the St Pancras Route's Corridor Expresses were timed to give impressively fast overall speeds. In those railway 'Golden Days' of 1910, the Route's crack train was the 13.30 Corridor for Glasgow. It made six calls en route but was allowed no more than 8hrs 50mins for the 426½ miles, giving an overall average of 48.3mph. This virtually matched the overall average speed of the West Coast Route's prestigious '2 o'clock Corridor' over its 401½ miles journey to Glasgow from Euston. The Settle & Carlisle 'leg' was formidable of course, but it has been presented sometimes as if its entire course of 72 miles was against the grade. In fact, once the northbound trains were over Ais Gill, there was that splendid long, downhill run on to Carlisle. The 13.30 Corridor was allowed 86mins only for its nonstop run of 77 miles from Hellifield – 54mph.

Before the 1914 War the St Pancras Route had an excellent service of Corridor Expresses and sleeping car trains to Glasgow and Edinburgh. There were good connections for Manchester and Liverpool via Hellifield and Backburn. Even after the 1923 Grouping the service was quite good, though friends of the old Midland Railway were convinced that the LNWR influence dominated the new London, Midland & Scottish Railway over the former Midland lines to the detriment of standards. In 1927 the LMS introduced many 'Titled Trains' and two of these were for the St Pancras Route: the *Thames-Clyde Express* and the *Thames-Forth Express*. These trains did something to restore the standards attained by the Corridors. The *Thames-Clyde Express* had to make eight calls but it still had the excellent journey time of 8hrs 38mins for the 424½ miles from St Pancras to Glasgow – an overall average of 49mph. But once the East and West Coast

Routes ended their minimum journey-time agreement, the St Pancras Route was altogether eclipsed for speed. By 1937-38 the best times over the rival routes were brought down to just 7hrs (with 6hrs for the LNER's *Coronation* and 6½hrs for the LMS's *Coronation Scot* lightly-loaded superfliers).

During the 1939-45 War, the St Pancras Route carried heavy military traffic, despite the inevitable problems of maintenance, but the war could hardly be blamed for the subsequent decline of the Route. Understandably, nationalisation led to re-appraisal of the investment implications of continuing to operate three Anglo-Scottish routes and it was no surprise when, in 1963, the Beeching Report proposed withdrawal of all passenger services between Settle and Carlisle. Nor was there later a realistic basis for regarding the St Pancras Route as a viable proposition for electrification. It was sad, nonetheless, to come to those years when the restored *Thames-Clyde Express* had 9¼-9¾hrs for its journey to Glasgow. It was sadder still when, in 1976, the one remaining through train between London and Glasgow was withdrawn. That wholly inadequate substitute of a through train between Nottingham and Glasgow was short-lived – it came to an end in 1982, leaving the Settle & Carlisle Line with only a 'local' passenger service between Leeds and Carlisle.

It is not possible in the space available here to make proper mention of the operation of the St Pancras Route and its motive power and rolling stock. That giant of Victorian Locomotive Superintendents, Samuel Waite Johnson, dominated the scene for 30 years until 1903 and he set his stamp on the Route and on performance over the Settle & Carlisle Line. His 4-4-0 engines of the 1890s with their simple, clean-cut lines, were as handsome as any engines designed in Britain and they met the challenge of the Settle & Carlisle with great success. Later, the Midland Compound 4-4-0s and their post-Grouping development provided the main-stay of the Route's motive power until the Stanier 4-6-0 Royal Scot engines came to work the Route. In the final phase, the Class 45 diesels were adequate for the work required.

The rise of the St Pancras Route owed a great deal to James Alport as General Manager of the Midland Railway and to Thomas Clayton as Carriage & Wagon Superintendent. It was Alport who transformed travel for the Third Class passenger when he abolished the Second Class and used its superior carriages for the third-class passengers. It was Alport also who brought Pullman luxury to Britain and Clayton modelled his admirable bogie 12-wheel, clerestoried carriages for the Route in 1875-76 on the Pullman Cars assembled at Derby from parts imported from the USA. What a wonderful experience it must have been for those first travellers over the Settle & Carlisle Line to enjoy the scenery and engineering from the comfort of such carriages! There is no doubt that in the summer of 1914 the St Pancras Route gave its passengers the most comfortable travel available in Britain and this applied to both its first and third-class passengers.

As I write these notes, the future of the Settle & Carlisle Line is not yet fully assured. It is a great mercy that the Line has been kept open since the final downgrading in 1982 and so made available many exciting journeys behind famous preserved steam locomotives. We must hope that the great and gallant efforts made to secure a long-term future for the Line will be crowned with success. It would be a tragic loss if this remarkable part of the British railway heritage became just another piece of industrial archaeology – as in the sad case of its Scottish counterpart, the Waverley Line.

Neil Caplan,
Cuckfield, Sussex

© January 1989

2. *Above* A delightful scene at Kirkby Stephen West on 1 December
1965 as the stationmaster pulls a single ticket for Garsdale prior to
the evening departure of the Carlisle-Bradford stopping train.
MAURICE BURNS

3. *Right* On 13 May 1961 Royal Scot Class 4-6-0 No 46117 *Welsh Guardsman* is seen approaching Ais Gill summit with the up *Thames-Clyde Express* bound for London St Pancras. This, together with the *Waverley*, were the two principal trains on the route, the *Thames-Clyde* serving Glasgow, and the *Waverley* serving Edinburgh. Both trains originated from St Pancras. ROBERT LESLIE

4. *Above* A vintage diesel scene taken in July 1967. Peak No D23 (original numbering) leaves Birkett tunnel with the 0950 Edinburgh-St Pancras *The Waverley*.

The first section of the journey would have been over the famous Waverley route, sadly closed in 1969. PETER J. ROBINSON

5. *Above* On 1 April 1989, Southern Railway Merchant Navy Pacific No 35028 *Clan Line* crosses Eden Lacy viaduct (north of Appleby) with the northbound *Cumbrian Mountain Express*. RS

6. *Opposite* In July 1967 Class 5 4-6-0 No 44767 (now happily preserved and named *George Stephenson*) is climbing up to Ais Gill with a heavy southbound mineral train. This locomotive is fitted with Stephenson link motion (outside) and Timken roller bearings.
MICK YORK

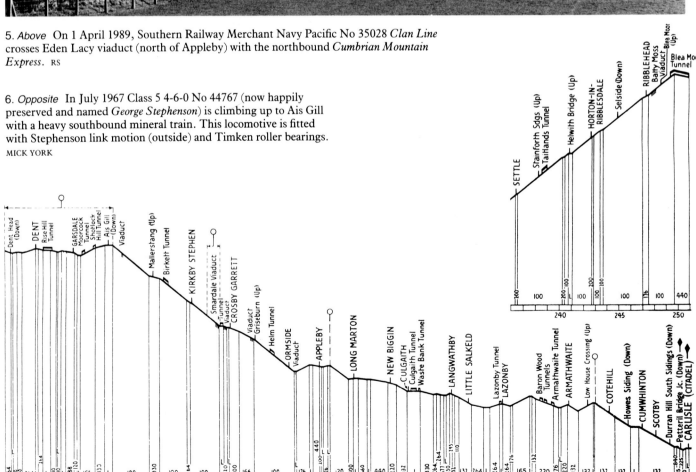

MILE POST MILEAGE

12

PART ONE
The Memories of Working Steam

7. *Above* Apart from 11 August 1968, the last steam working on
the S & C was supposed to be on 31 December 1967. However, on
31 May 1968 Standard Class 4MT No 75019 worked a special
ballast train from the quarry on the Grassington branch (near
Skipton) to Appleby.

    The train here is seen climbing out of Horton in Ribblesdale.
MICK YORK

8. *Right* Britannia Pacific No 70029 (formerly *Shooting Star*)
approaches Ribblehead station on 18 April 1967 with the 1255
Hunslet (Leeds)-Carlisle freight. From Settle junction, northbound
trains faced a 15-mile climb of around 1 in 100 up to Blea Moor
tunnel where the line undulates for around 10 miles to Ais Gill from
where, apart from short sections, it is down grade all the way to
Carlisle, some 48 miles from Ais Gill. GAVIN MORRISON

9. *Right* Class 4F 0-6-0 No 44094 ambles over Dent Head viaduct on a summer afternoon in 1955 with a southbound goods. ERIC TREACY/MILLBROOK HOUSE

10. *Below* Fowler 2-6-4T No 42313 accelerates out of Armathwaite with the 1805 Carlisle-Appleby stopping train. 5 June 1962. ROBERT LESLIE

11. *Opposite* A southbound freight headed by Class 5 4-6-0 No 44675 gives out a wonderful exhaust as it climbs out of Birkett tunnel on a bright April morning in 1967. The train still has 4 miles of around 1 in 100 before Ais Gill summit is reached. From Ormside (where the 'Long Drag' really starts) to Ais Gill is a distance of 15 miles at around 1 in 100, a stiff task for any locomotive. MAURICE BURNS

Overleaf
12. *Left* A sight to gladden any steam enthusiast, an 8F on the Settle & Carlisle.

2-8-0 No 48090 toils up the steep grades near Kirkby Stephen with a southbound goods, 4 November 1967. KEN HALE

13. *Right* Jubilee No 45593 *Kolhapur* in the Mallerstang valley, north of Ais Gill, working its passage back to Leeds with the 0945 Carlisle-Stourton freight on an August Monday in 1967. The locomotive had worked the relief to the northbound *Thames-Clyde Express* the previous Saturday. At this time the engine was shedded at Leeds Holbeck (55A). S. C. CROOK

14. *Above* The 1637 Carlisle-Bradford stopping train passing Cumwhinton in August 1965 behind BR Standard Class Pacific No 72008 *Clan Macleod.* (The station is just to the far side of the bridge.) S. C. CROOK

15. *Top* Jubilee Class 4-6-0 No 45562 *Alberta* brightens a dull day as it heads north through Stainforth on 5 August 1967 with the 0640 Birmingham-Glasgow train. C. E. WESTON

16. *Bottom* On 11 August 1968 (the last day of steam on British Railways) Class 5s Nos 44781 and 44871 head south off Ribblehead viaduct with the return *Fifteen Guinea Special* from Liverpool/ Manchester to Carlisle (via the S & C) and return. The northbound trip on the S & C being worked by Britannia Pacific No 70013 *Oliver Cromwell*. MICK YORK

17. 18. Two views of *Oliver Cromwell* on an early Sunday morning in April 1967 as it approaches and passes Blea Moor signalbox with a return football special back from Wembley to Scotland on the occasion of an England v Scotland match. Note the water tower. MICK YORK

19. *Left.* Class 4F 0-6-0
No 44007 (with tender
cab) is seen in charge of a
Durran Hill-Skipton
goods on 3 May 1958.
The location is near Low
House crossing. These
0-6-0s were introduced in
1911 and designed by
Fowler for the Midland
Railway. ROBERT LESLIE

20. *Above* In BR steam days, locomotives from other regions were no strangers to the S & C route – even GWR engines. On 30 September 1967 Castle Class 4-6-0 No 7029 *Clun Castle* (now happily preserved at Tyseley) makes a fine sight as it climbs the 1 in 100 at Stainforth with the northbound A4 Locomotive Society railtour from Peterborough to Carlisle. KEN HALE

Opposite

21. *Top right* Another view of the previous train, this time as it approaches Dent station. LES NIXON

22. *Bottom right* *Clun Castle* glints in the evening sunshine as it leaves Carlisle (near Durran Hill) with a return excursion to Hellifield and Liverpool. The outward journey was via Preston and the West Coast main line, No 7029 being the motive power for this section also. This trip was organised by the Locomotive Club of Great Britain (LCGB). 14th October 1967. KEN HALE

23. *Opposite* Jubilee 4-6-0 No 45697 *Achilles* near Cumwhinton at the start of its climb to Ais Gill with CTAC Scottish Tours Express charter train from Glasgow to Leicester. 7 August 1965. PETER J. ROBINSON

24. *Above* On 13 February 1965 Royal Scot 4-6-0 No 46115 *Scots Guardsman* approaches Ribblehead station with a special Scot Commemorative tour from Crewe to Carlisle via the S & C and return via Shap. This tour was organised by the Railway Correspondence & Travel Society (RCTS). *Scots Guardsman* was the last member of this illustrious class to be withdrawn but has happily been preserved at Dinting. GAVIN MORRISON

25. *Above* Another Royal Scot, No 46103 *Royal Scots Fusilier*, hurries through Armathwaite with the 1600 Glasgow-Leeds train on 5 July 1958. Note the amount of sidings and the smart-looking goods shed, a sign of more prosperous times on the S & C.   ROBERT LESLIE

26. *Above* To complete this trio of Royal Scots we see No 46109 *Royal Engineer* in charge of the northbound *Waverley* in a classic setting – the approach to Dent station with Arten Gill viaduct in the background. At a height of around 1,000 feet, Dent is the highest station in England, hence the necessity of snow fences on the left-hand side. The date of this picture is June 1959. ERIC TREACY/MILLBROOK HOUSE

27. *Above* Crab 2-6-0 No 42790, with an up freight, passes through a typical Midland station – Cumwhinton, 16 July 1955. Cumwhinton is some 4 miles to the south of Carlisle. Of particular note is the LMS poster on the left-hand station buildings, advertising the beauties of Loch Lomond. ROBERT LESLIE

28. *Top right* Jubilee 4-6-0 No 45573 *Newfoundland* climbs up to Ais Gill with the CTAC Scottish tours special from Gourock to Leicester, 17 July 1965. MAURICE BURNS

29. *Bottom right* On a pleasant afternoon, 19 October 1957, former LMS Class 4F 0-6-0 No 44584 of Stourton shed (55B) trundles along near Armathwaite tunnel with a Durran Hill-Skipton mixed freight. ROBERT LESLIE

30. *Above* On 17 July 1965 Clan Pacific No 72008 *Clan Macleod*
pauses at Garsdale station with an afternoon Skipton-Carlisle
stopping train. Garsdale was the junction for the Midland line to
Hawes which connected with the North Eastern line to
Northallerton. Originally Garsdale was known as Hawes Junction
& Garsdale. MAURICE BURNS

31. *Right* The highest water troughs in the country were situated
just south of Garsdale station. On 12 August 1967 Jubilee 4-6-0
No 45562 *Alberta* races across the troughs with the 0640
Birmingham-Glasgow train. This impressive picture was taken
from the top of the water tower and shows to good advantage the
picturesque Pennine scenery. KEN HALE

33. *Above* In September 1965 an unidentified Class 5 locomotive pulls through Armathwaite with a northbound goods.
MAURICE BURNS

32. *Left* This picture is reputed to have been one of Eric Treacy's favourites and it is easy to see why. Jubilee No 45573 *Newfoundland* is seen climbing up to Ais Gill summit with the up *Waverley* express. Wild Boar Fell dominates the background.
ERIC TREACY/MILLBROOK HOUSE

34. *Above* An Ivatt Class 4MT 2-6-0 pulls across Long Marton
viaduct with a northbound goods in late May 1965. The hill in the
background is Dufton Pike. MAURICE BURNS

35. *Right* No 45593 *Kolhapur* in charge of the 0920 St Pancras-
Glasgow, climbs the 1 in 100 just north of Settle, 5 August 1967.
C. E. WESTON

36. *Top* On 29 April 1967 Class 8F No 48421 is pictured near Smardale with an up soda-ash train. The freight has just crossed Smardale viaduct (which is on the level) and is now climbing the 1 in 100 up to Kirkby Stephen. LES NIXON

37. *Above* In the summer of 1955, 4F 0-6-0 No 43922 plus an unidentified 8F are seen with a very lengthy freight approaching Helwith Bridge some 6 miles to the north of Settle junction.
ERIC TREACY/MILLBROOK HOUSE

38. *Top* In the last few years of BR steam many locomotives appeared to be in a run-down condition yet 9F 2-10-0 No 92018, although looking the worse for wear, seems to be in no trouble at all as it approaches Ais Gill summit with a southbound iron ore train, 13 September 1966. This locomotive was built at Crewe in 1954 and withdrawn in April 1967. RS

39. *Above* Another locomotive in poor external condition and yet seemingly in no trouble is Jubilee No 45675 *Hardy*, photographed in October 1966 as it storms through Dent station with an up fitted freight. LES NIXON

40. *Top left* Britannia Pacific No 70039 (formerly *Sir Christopher Wren*) passes Kirkby Stephen with a returning Edinburgh to Cardiff rugby supporters' special, 5 February 1967. Note the high semaphore signal for sighting purposes. GAVIN MORRISON

41. *Bottom left* On 9 April 1960 Britannia No 70044 *Earl Haig* is seen at speed just to the north of Low House crossing with the 1035 Leeds-Glasgow train. Low House crossing box can be seen on the right-hand side of the picture. The only other crossing on the route is at Culgaith some 8 miles to the north of Appleby and 15 miles to the south of Low House crossing. ROBERT LESLIE

42. *Above* Saturday 4 July 1964 sees No 70002 *Geoffrey Chaucer* in charge of the up relief *Waverley*. The location is the cutting just south of Birkett tunnel. GAVIN MORRISON

Overleaf

43. *Left* In the late 1950s and early 1960s former LNER A3 Pacifics were not an uncommon sight on the S & C working service and special trains.
   No 60072 *Sunstar* makes a splendid sight as it storms out of Carlisle past Petteril Bridge junction with the up *Thames-Clyde Express* in January 1961. Petteril Bridge is the junction for the line to Newcastle. S. C. CROOK

44. *Right* Class 8F No 48074 struggles up the last few yards to Blea Moor with a down freight on a bitterly cold morning, 4 November 1967. This is a beautiful picture and one which captures the magic of the line. GAVIN MORRISON

45. 46. 47. Three scenes taken in 1965 which describe so well the character of this Pennine route. MAURICE BURNS

48. *Left* On 12 August 1967, Class 8F 2-8-0 No 48517 and
9F 2-10-0 No 92137 climb over Lunds viaduct with a train of rails.
This location is a mile to the north of Garsdale and the rear of the
train is still in the short Moorcock tunnel. KEN HALE

49. *Top* Class 5MT 2-6-0 No 42774 makes a fine sight as it heads
south through Dent with a mixed freight in the 1950s. Note the
neat-looking station signalbox and sidings and, completing a very
rural scene, a cattle dock. ERIC TREACY/MILLBROOK HOUSE

50. *Above* A pair of 9F 2-10-0s led by No 92125 provide super
power for a very long rail train and are pictured heading north
through Dent, July 1967. MICK YORK

51. *Above* Although in 1967 Jubilee 4-6-0s worked many passenger trains over the S & C, these were mainly confined to summer Saturdays and on weekdays these handsome locomotives were to be found on many goods trains. Such was the case on 30 September 1967 as No 45562 *Alberta* heads northwards through Stainforth with the 1330 Leeds-Carlisle goods. KEN HALE

52. *Top right* Another view of *Alberta* (in earlier days), this time in its more usual role as a top-class express locomotive. No 45562 is seen at Ais Gill summit with the up *Waverley*, 13 May 1961. ROBERT LESLIE

53. *Bottom right* Finally, we see *Alberta* in its other role in 1967 on a summer Saturday express – the 0640 Birmingham-Glasgow. The location is Blea Moor with Ingleborough in the background, and the date 19 August. KEN HALE

54. *Top left* On a very wet spring day, 6 May 1967, 9F 2-10-0 No 92421 makes an all-out effort as it tops Ais Gill summit with a southbound ore train from Long Meg sidings. KEN HALE

55. *Bottom left* Class 5 4-6-0 No 45426 makes heavy weather of the climb to Ais Gill summit with a southbound fitted freight in December 1965. MAURICE BURNS

56. *Above* The town of Settle and the surrounding valley look very picturesque after a heavy fall of snow on 1 December 1965. In the middle distance a Class 5 locomotive heads north with a three-coach local train. The S & C line is attractive in all seasons but on a true winter's day, with a layer of snow, it arguably looks at its finest. MAURICE BURNS

57. *Above* A scene from the early 1950s as Class 4F 0-6-0 No 43902 heads north through Dent with a PW train.
ERIC TREACY/MILLBROOK HOUSE

58. *Top right* Another vintage scene as Class 5 No 44755 (complete with Caprotti valve gear) heads south away from Ais Gill summit in 1958.

For the next 10 miles to Blea Moor the line is undulating and from then on it is all down grade for southbound trains.
ERIC TREACY/MILLBROOK HOUSE

59. *Bottom right* Ex-Crosti boilered 9F 2-10-0 No 92021 approaches Ribblehead station on 5 August 1967 with a northbound freight. The line to Ribblehead quarry can be seen in the foreground.
GAVIN MORRISON

60. *Above* A spectacular view of the southern entrance to Blea Moor tunnel taken from the footplate of A3 Pacific No 60081 *Shotover* on a northbound express in the late 1950s. Note the length of Blea Moor tunnel: 2,629 yards. ERIC TREACY/MILLBROOK HOUSE

61. *Top right* 4-6-0 No 75019 crosses Ribblehead viaduct on 31 May 1968 with a ballast train from the Grassington branch to Appleby. KEN HALE

62. *Centre right* A broadside view of 9F 2-10-0 No 92082 as it heads north in charge of a mixed freight, 4 November 1967. The location is just north of Helwith Bridge where the line follows closely the valley of the River Ribble. In the background is Beecroft quarry. LES NIXON

63. *Bottom right* Class 8F 2-8-0 No 48074 has just left Dandry Mire viaduct, Garsdale, and is seen heading north for Carlisle with a goods train, 4 November 1967. The train is crossing over the A684, the Sedbergh-Hawes road. LES NIXON

64. *Top left* A vintage scene at Langwathby on 3 November 1956 as 4F 0-6-0 No 43896 is shunting wagons of gypsum rock. The fireman is having a driving lesson under the watchful eye of the driver! ROBERT LESLIE

65. *Bottom left* Clan Pacific No 72005 *Clan Macgregor* with the 1135 Hellifield-Carlisle at Armathwaite viaduct, 27 January 1962. The line here closely follows the course of the River Eden. ROBERT LESLIE

66. *Above* On 7 October 1967 Jubilee 4-6-0 No 45562 *Alberta* rounds Smardale curve with *The South Yorkshireman* railtour. MAURICE BURNS

Overleaf

67. *Top left* Carlisle Citadel station in 1957. Royal Scot 4-6-0 No 46136 *The Border Regiment* receives attention before taking out a southbound express.

Behind the Scot is Jubilee No 45564 *New South Wales*, and behind the Jubilee is an up express with what appears to be an A3 Pacific in charge, in which case it is probably bound for Leeds via the S & C. ERIC TREACY/MILLBROOK HOUSE

68. *Bottom left* Carlisle Citadel on the same day as the previous picture. Jubilee No 45564 *New South Wales* makes a smart departure with an up express. ERIC TREACY/MILLBROOK HOUSE

69. *Top right* For many years the Class 2P 4-4-0s were regular performers on the S & C. In this scene, taken around 1949, we see 2P No 40615 double-headed with a Jubilee 4-6-0 on probably the up *Thames-Clyde Express*. The train has just left Carlisle station and the West Coast main line can be clearly seen on the left-hand side of the picture. Within a mile at Petteril Bridge junction the Newcastle line will head due east and the S & C line will head south-east for Appleby. ERIC TREACY/MILLBROOK HOUSE

70. *Bottom right* Class 5 4-6-0 No 44899 and Jubilee No 45568 *Western Australia* leave Carlisle on the up *Waverley*, 24 January 1959. ROBERT LESLIE

73. *Above* On 30 April 1967 Class 9F 2-10-0 No 92051 makes a very pleasant sight as it pulls out of Appleby with a southbound train of anhydrite from Long Meg sidings, just north of Little Salkeld. LES NIXON

71. *Top left* Royal Scot 4-6-0 No 46117 *Welsh Guardsman* toils uphill over Griseburn viaduct, south of Appleby, with the up *Waverley* on 20 August 1960. This short seven-arch viaduct spans Potts Beck. ROBERT LESLIE

72. *Bottom left* Ex-LNER A3 Pacific No 60082 *Neil Gow* at speed in the lovely Eden Valley at Baron Wood, between Lazonby and Armathwaite, with the down *Thames-Clyde Express*. 20 August 1960. ROBERT LESLIE

74. *Top* On a very hot summer's day in 1955 Class 4F No 44315 trundles through Dent with a down ore train.
ERIC TREACY/MILLBROOK HOUSE

75. *Bottom* Class A3 4-6-2 No 4472 *Flying Scotsman* hurries through Langwathby with a northbound excursion organised by the Gainsborough Model Railway Society, September 1967.
LES NIXON

76. *Above* Crab 2-6-0 No 42884 is framed by upper and lower quadrant signals as it heads south off Ribblehead viaduct with an up freight, probably around 1955.
ERIC TREACY/MILLBROOK HOUSE

77. *Left* On 15 July 1967 8F No 48111 heads north out of Lazonby with a heavy freight train bound for Carlisle. This picture was taken a mile or so north of Lazonby where the gradient is 1 in 165. KEN HALE

78. *Left* Britannia Pacific No 70009 (formerly *Alfred the Great*) approaches Ais Gill summit with a southbound goods, 13 September 1966. RS

79. *Bottom* A grimy Standard Class 4MT 4-6-0 No 75041 climbs up to Ais Gill with a Carlisle-Skipton freight, 13 September 1966. RS

80. *Top right* Class 4MT 2-6-0 No 43049 leaves Warcop and heads for Appleby with the return branch freight to Carlisle, 19 July 1967.

Although now known as the Warcop branch, this was originally the North Eastern line from Kirkby Stephen East via Appleby East to the LNWR main line at Eden Valley junction. All that now remains is the short section from Appleby to Warcop in order to serve the latter's army camp. KEN HALE

81. *Bottom right* Jubilee No 45593 *Kolhapur* heads over Dandry Mire viaduct at Garsdale with the 0920 St Pancras-Glasgow train on 12 August 1967. The track bed of the Hawes branch can be seen on the left-hand side. KEN HALE

82. *Top left* Standard 2-6-2T No 84015 passing over Garsdale troughs, high in the Pennines, with the 0712 Garsdale-Hellifield stopping train, 17 July 1965. MAURICE BURNS

83. *Bottom left* In the summer of 1958 Jubilee 4-6-0 No 45691 *Orion* is pictured passing Ribblehead quarry with a northbound mixed freight.
ERIC TREACY/MILLBROOK HOUSE

84. *Right* In lovely early evening light, Class 5 4-6-0 No 44857 rounds a curve near Armathwaite with a Durran Hill-Saltley freight, 17 May 1956. ROBERT LESLIE

85. *Below* 2-6-0 No 42881 on a Carlisle-Kings Norton (Birmingham) van train at Cotehill, 19 November 1960. ROBERT LESLIE

86. *Left* With the advent of the end of steam working over the S & C on 31 December 1967, many railtours were run in the autumn of that year.

One such tour was on 24 September, organised by the Midland area of the Stephenson Locomotive Society (SLS). The return trip with Britannia Pacific No 70013 *Oliver Cromwell* in charge is seen heading south near Cotehill. ROBERT LESLIE

87. *Bottom* Ex-Crosti boilered 9F 2-10-0 No 92022 (off Buxton shed 9D) approaches Ais Gill with a southbound goods on the morning of 17 July 1965. MAURICE BURNS

88. *Top right* Class 4F 0-6-0 No 44055, in ex-works condition, makes a fine sight as it speeds along near Cotehill with an up freight. 19 November 1960. ROBERT LESLIE

89. *Bottom right* On 15 February 1964 Crab 2-6-0 No 42831 heads south past Scotby with the 1305 Carlisle-Stourton goods. PETER J. ROBINSON

90. *Top* Britannia No 70029 (formerly *Shooting Star*) heads north between Settle junction and Settle with a Skipton-Carlisle goods, 18 April 1964. GAVIN MORRISON

91. *Above* The down *Thames-Clyde Express* headed by Britannia Pacific No 70053 *Moray Firth* makes an impressive looking sight as it approaches Blea Moor in the mid-1950s. These locomotives were first introduced in 1951 and this one was withdrawn in 1967. ERIC TREACY/MILLBROOK HOUSE

92. *Top* Another Britannia, this time No 70016 (formerly *Ariel*), leaving Birkett tunnel with the (SO) 0925 St Pancras-Glasgow St Enoch train, 22 July 1967. ROBERT LESLIE

93. *Above* Jubilee No 45562 *Alberta* passing Wild Boar Fell on an August Monday in 1967 on its return journey from working the down relief to the *Thames-Clyde Express* on the previous Saturday. S. C. CROOK

94. *Top* Rise Hill tunnel just north of Dent is the location as
4F 0-6-0 No 44208 heads south with a short mixed freight in 1960.
    This tunnel is roughly the boundary between the Garsdale
Valley (to the north) and Dent Dale. ERIC TREACY/MILLBROOK HOUSE

95. *Above* The 1637 Carlisle-Bradford stopping train approaches
Low House crossing, near Armathwaite, hauled by Class 5 4-6-0
No 44668, 18 August 1959. ROBERT LESLIE

96. *Top* The scene at Ais Gill summit on 11 August 1968 as
No 70013 *Oliver Cromwell* waits to leave with the *Fifteen Guinea
Special* to Carlisle.

Note the number of cars parked on the Kirkby Stephen road
(right-hand side); they were parked almost to the Moorcock Inn,
some three miles south of here! RS

97. *Above* The final picture in this section shows the return *Fifteen
Guinea Special* as it approaches Soulby, hauled by Class 5s
Nos 44781 and 44871. LES NIXON

98. *Right* On the evening of 23 April 1984, Class 47/4 No 47481 leaves Armathwaite viaduct with the 1600 Leeds-Carlisle service. This graceful curving viaduct has nine arches and is 176 yards long. RS

PART TWO
The Power of the Diesels

99. *Top* A rare meeting of Class 37s on the S & C, 2 May 1987. No 37178 of Eastfield depot is on standby duty, whilst the diverted northbound *Cornishman* (0730 Penzance-Aberdeen) passes with No 37135 in charge. GAVIN MORRISON

100. *Above* A distinguished visitor to the S & C on 14 November 1981 was Deltic No 55009 *Alycidon* with the northbound *Deltic Cumbrian* railtour. Even the S & C scenery at Dent fails to dwarf the size of these powerful locomotives. Fortunately, this locomotive is preserved on the North Yorkshire Moors Railway. GAVIN MORRISON

Previous page

101. *Top* Since the introduction of diesel traction on the Settle & Carlisle in the early 1960s, the main motive power (until their recent withdrawal) for the principal passenger trains has been the Class 45s or Peaks. This was certainly the case on 21 April 1984 as Class 45/1 No 45150 powers its way past Dent Station with the 1040 Carlisle-Leeds train. RS

102. *Bottom* Horton-in-Ribblesdale is the setting as Peak No 45142 in charge of the 0907 Leeds-Carlisle train powers its way northwards, 20 April 1984.

The sidings on the right serve the nearby Beecroft Quarries. The tall semaphore signals (for sighting purposes) have now disappeared but the signal box still remains. RS

103. *Left* On 30 September 1983 Class 25 No 25239 approaches the Midland signalbox at Appleby with the morning Warcop branch train from Carlisle. The train will pause in the station before reversing down the line to Appleby East and then southwards to Warcop. RS

104. *Bottom* Class 31/4 No 31406 speeds through Howes sidings on 16 August 1983 with the 1640 Carlisle-Leeds train. The entrance to the sidings (which by this time had been taken up) can be seen on the left-hand side. RS

105. *Above* The gracefully curving Smardale viaduct is the setting as a special excursion from North Walsingham to Carlisle hauled by Class 47/4 No 47487 heads north, 21 April 1984. This viaduct is 237 yards long (second longest on the line) has 12 spans and crosses Scandal Beck as well as the track bed of the North Eastern line from Kirkby Stephen to Tebay on the WCML. RS

106. *Above* On 9 May 1982 the diverted 0726 Carlisle-Euston
hauled by Class 47/4 No 47455 crosses Arten Gill viaduct a mile or
so south of Dent station. PETER J. ROBINSON

107. *Top right* Class 45/0 No 45020 powers its way over Ais Gill
viaduct with the 1640 Carlisle-Leeds train, 24 April 1984. RS

108. *Bottom right* Peak No 45132 crosses the short (110 yards) but
elegant viaduct at Crosby Garrett with a return Carlisle-Leicester
special excursion, 21 April 1984. RS

109. *Top* One of the great features of the S & C is the railway architecture.

On 22 April 1984, Class 40 No 40060 in charge of the Glasgow-Red Bank (Manchester) van train passes by a splendid example of a MR signalbox at Culgaith crossing. A northbound train can be seen disappearing into Culgaith tunnel (661 yards long). RS

110. *Above* The former Midland station at Kirkby Stephen is the setting as a Carlisle-Kings Cross excursion hurries through with Class 40 No 40012 in charge, 13 October 1984. RS

111. *Top* Note the box at Garsdale, situated on the down platform of the station. On 4 May 1985, Class 47/4 No 47555 passes through in charge of a diverted morning Nottingham-Glasgow service. RS

112. *Above* Class 40 No 40086 pauses at the fine-looking former NE station at Appleby East, 8 October 1984.

The train, which has just returned from Warcop, is an Edinburgh-Keighley excursion. TOM HEAVYSIDE

113. *Top left* On Saturday, 4 November 1967, English Electric Type 4 (Class 40) No D393 approaches the road bridge which carries the B6259 to Kirkby Stephen as it heads south with a mixed freight near Ais Gill. GAVIN MORRISON

114. *Bottom left* Class 45 No 45059 *Royal Engineer* heads the up *Thames-Clyde Express* across Dent Head viaduct, 18 May 1975. ROBERT LESLIE

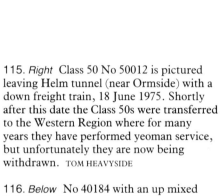

115. *Right* Class 50 No 50012 is pictured leaving Helm tunnel (near Ormside) with a down freight train, 18 June 1975. Shortly after this date the Class 50s were transferred to the Western Region where for many years they have performed yeoman service, but unfortunately they are now being withdrawn. TOM HEAVYSIDE

116. *Below* No 40184 with an up mixed freight climbs through the Mallerstang valley on the approach to Ais Gill, 2 September 1981. RS

117. *Left* A relic of the past at Lazonby: a water crane. Class 47/4 No 47434 approaches the station with the diverted 0950 Glasgow-Euston on Sunday, 22 April 1984. Note the goods shed on the left-hand side, now used by a local bakery. RS

118. *Above* No mistaking the shape of a Class 40 (No 40082) as it trundles over Long Marton viaduct with a return pick-up freight from Appleby to Carlisle, 24 April 1984. This viaduct crosses over Trout Beck, a tributary of the River Eden. RS

119. *Top left* A delightful winter scene at Garsdale, 3 March 1984, as Class 47/4 No 47529 heads north with an LNER society excursion to Carlisle.
PETER J. ROBINSON

120. *Bottom left* In the winter of 1970 the diverted 1100 Glasgow-Birmingham service hauled by Class 50 No D417 makes a fine sight as it nears Ais Gill summit.
    Prior to electrification Class 50s were regular performers on the WCML and only occasionally on the S & C. PETER J. ROBINSON

121. *Right* A raw winter's day at Kirkby Stephen as Class 31/4 No 31411 hurries north with the morning Leeds-Carlisle service, 12 February 1982. The semaphores are worthy of note, the posts providing a contrast between old and new.
TOM HEAVYSIDE

122. *Below* Class 45/1 No 45142 approaches Garsdale with the 0907 Leeds-Carlisle train, 3 March 1984. PETER J. ROBINSON

These four pictures, taken on true winter days, show the Settle and Carlisle at its most picturesque and remind us that whatever the weather the train can usually get through.

123. *Top left* A lovely late spring day at Smardale as Class 47/4 No 47477 heads north with a SLOA Kings Cross-Carlisle excursion, 10 May 1986. The return will be by steam power: Class 5 No 5305.

In the foreground are a typical dales farmhouse and buildings and fine dry stone walls. LES NIXON

124. *Bottom left* A beautiful view looking down Dent Dale as Peak No 45133 passes through Dent station with the 1605 Leeds-Carlisle train, 29 May 1982. TOM HEAVYSIDE

125. *Above* Peak No D23 in early BR livery glints in the afternoon sunshine as it heads the up *Thames-Clyde Express* through Dent in 1966. LES NIXON

126. *Above* An almost aerial view of Smardale as Peak No 45150 hurries over Crosby Garrett viaduct with the 1600 Leeds-Carlisle service, 21 April 1984. Beyond the back of the train can be seen the entrance to the short Crosby Garrett tunnel, at the other end of which is situated Smardale viaduct. RS

127. *Top right* On 30 September 1983, Class 25 No 25239 is busy shunting at Warcop before returning to Carlisle with the empty vans. The line now terminates here but originally carried on to Kirkby Stephen (East). RS

128. *Bottom right* Class 40 No D200 approaches Howes siding on a very pleasant evening, 16 August 1983, with the 1600 Leeds-Carlisle train. This preserved Class 40 has been a regular performer on the S & C in the last few years. RS

129. *Top* Peak No 45142 accelerates out of Appleby on 20 April 1984 with the 1640 Carlisle-Leeds train and approaches a fine-looking semaphore signal complete with a MR wooden post and finial. RS

130. *Above* The Midland Railway box at Howe & Co's sidings (five miles south of Carlisle) provides a contrast with D200 (No 40122) as it rushes by with the 1040 Carlisle-Leeds service, 24 August 1983. RS

131. 132. *Above* Nocturne at Appleby, 9 December 1983.
    In the top view we see No 45137 *The Bedfordshire and Hertfordshire Regiment (TA)* with the 1640 Carlisle-Leeds.
    The lower scene shows No 47446 with the 1600 Leeds-Carlisle train. Note the Midland Hotel, a famous landmark for travellers on the S & C. RS

133. *Top right* Jubilee No 5593 *Kolhapur* looks a treat as it hurries south with the *Mancunian* on 18 April 1987. The location is Durran Hill, Carlisle, site of the former Midland Railway shed. RS

134. *Bottom right* On 10 August 1989, Jubilee Class 4-6-0 No 45596 *Bahamas* is seen heading northwards through Baron Wood on its first outing over the line since the 1960s. Appropriately, the locomotive is in BR Green livery and the carriages in maroon. RS

PART THREE
In Praise of Preserved Steam

137. *Above* *Flying Scotsman* storms up the 1 in 165 to Shotlock Hill tunnel with a York-Carlisle special, 4 May 1987. The Kirkby Stephen road (on the left-hand side) is unusually clear of cars, a rare event on a 'special' day. RS

135. *Top left* Lunds viaduct is the setting as LMS Coronation Class Pacific No 46229 *Duchess of Hamilton* heads north with a special train, 10 August 1982. LES NIXON

136. *Bottom left* Southern Railway 4-6-0 No 850 *Lord Nelson* glows in the winter sunshine as it heads north off Garsdale viaduct on 24 January 1981 with the *Cumbrian Mountain Express*. LES NIXON

138. *Top left* A distinguished visitor from north of the border was A4 Pacific No 60009 *Union of South Africa*. 'No 9' (as it is known) is seen speeding south with a CME, 31 March 1984. The location is Newbiggin just south of Culgaith. RS

139. *Bottom left* Double heading of special trains is quite rare on the S & C but on 26 July 1987, LNER Class K1 2-6-0 No 2005 and LMS Class 5 No 5305 provide super power for the northbound *North Eastern* special. The train is just leaving Shotlock Hill tunnel which is located about a mile south of Ais Gill summit. RS

140. *Right* On 30 May, the popular and powerful *Duchess of Hamilton* is seen at Newbiggin knocking another 12secs off her record time of 23mins 55secs, from Appleby to Ais Gill, which she had achieved on 19 March. The blue ribbon and plaque on the front commemorate this feat. No 46229 was withdrawn for general overhaul in November 1985, but is now back in service again. RS

141. *Below* After an absence of some ten years, Merchant Navy Pacific No 35028 *Clan Line* returned to the line again. On its return on 10 December 1988, No 35028 is seen heading northwards near Stainforth with *The Pennine Limited*. RS

143. *Above* No 46229 provides a superb spectacle as it heads north off Dandry Mire viaduct (Garsdale) with the *Thames-Clyde Express* from Leeds to Newcastle, 23 March 1985. LES NIXON

142. *Left* Former SR 4-6-0 No 777 *Sir Lamiel* makes a fine sight as it heads north on a *Santa Steam Special*, 27 December 1984. The location is just south of Appleby. The remarkable cloud formation is caused by the famous Helm Wind. ROBERT LESLIE

144. *Top left* A view from the buffer stops at Garsdale of the rear of a Leeds-Carlisle special, 8 March 1986. The motive power is provided by Class 5 4-6-0 No 5305. LES NIXON

145. *Bottom left* The last steam locomotive built by BR, 9F 2-10-0 No 92220 *Evening Star* is seen heading over Long Marton viaduct with the southbound CME, 23 April 1984. RS

146. *Above* This picture was taken from by the side of the little chapel that lies below Garsdale viaduct.

No 60009 *Union of South Africa* heads off the viaduct with the northbound CMP, 20 April 1984. RS

147. 148. *Above and left* Two pictures, taken at roughly the same location, of trains not quite on the S & C but within a few feet of it. The location is the approach to Settle junction and the top view, taken on 10 August 1975, shows GWR Hall Class 4-6-0 No 6960 *Raveningham Hall* and LNER B1 4-6-0 No 1306 *Mayflower* as they head off the Carnforth line bound for Darlington for the Stockton & Darlington celebrations. In the lower view 7F 2-8-0 No 53809 heads south with *The West Yorkshire Limited* on the evening of 16 August 1986. The S & C route can be seen clearly heading away northwards at the rear of the train. RS

149. *Top right* A pugnacious looking *Lord Nelson* thunders through Dent, 31 July 1980, with the southbound CME. The road bridge carries the famous 'coal road' between Dent and Garsdale, which is often blocked with snow in wintertime. GAVIN MORRISON

150. *Bottom right* Former North British Railway 0-6-0 No 673 *Maude* is seen near Arten Gill with a special from Kilmarnock to Manchester for the Rainhill celebrations, 17 May 1980. LES NIXON

151. *Above* Saturday, 25 March 1978 saw the return of steam working on the S & C line after an absence of ten years. The first special was *The Norfolkman* hauled by LNER V2 Class 2-6-2 No 4771 *Green Arrow*. The weather is decidedly wintry as can be seen from this shot of No 4771 with the northbound special as it struggles up the 1 in 100 near Helwith Bridge. GAVIN MORRISON

152. *Top right* On 12 February 1983 Midland Compound 4-4-0 No 1000 and Jubilee 4-6-0 No 5960 *Leander* head round the curve at Armathwaite with the southbound CMP. RS

153. *Bottom right Flying Scotsman* tops Ais Gill in fine style on 30 January 1983 with a southbound special excursion for SLOA (Steam Locomotive Operations Association). RS

154. *Top* Class 5 4-6-0 No 44767 *George Stephenson* heads the down CME at Smardale viaduct, 5 July 1984. ROBERT LESLIE

155. *Above* No 35028 *Clan Line* approaches Birkett tunnel on 30 September 1978 with a return special working from the memorial service held at Appleby for Bishop Eric Treacy. GAVIN MORRISON

156. *Top* On 20 September 1984, No 46229 is seen near Birkett tunnel with a southbound CME. RS

157. *Above* The northern exit from Blea Moor tunnel is the location as 8F 2-8-0 No 48151 heads a northbound excursion, 25 June 1988. RS

158. *Top left* No 5690 *Leander* approaches Shotlock Hill tunnel on
26 April 1980 with a Hellifield-Carlisle special. TOM HEAVYSIDE

159. *Bottom left* 29 October 1988 was a glorious day on the S & C,
the sun shone for most of the time and Stanier 8F No 48151 was in
charge of a northbound special. What a combination! The special is
seen in lovely light just south of Ais Gill summit. Note the beautiful
dry stone walls, such a characteristic feature of this part of the world.

RS

160. *Above* A classic setting for a Jubilee locomotive as No 5593
climbs the 1 in 100 over Ais Gill viaduct with the southbound
Mancunian, 18 April 1987. RS

161. *Top left* A rare visitor to the S & C is LMS 4-6-2 No 6201 *Princess Elizabeth*.

This elegant Pacific locomotive is seen near Eden Lacy viaduct with a Blackburn-Carlisle special, 25 July 1987. RS

162. *Bottom left* A regular performer on the line is Gresley A4 Pacific No 4498 *Sir Nigel Gresley*. The locomotive is seen in charge of a northbound special at Ais Gill summit on 13 October 1984. To the right of the train is where the sidings and summit signalbox were located. RS

163. 164 *Right and below* Another reliable and regular locomotive on the S & C is SR 4-6-2 No 34092 *City of Wells* (based at the Keighley and Worth Valley Railway). In the top view, taken on 13 February 1982, No 34092 is seen near Armathwaite with a southbound special.

In the bottom view the West Country Pacific, complete with *Golden Arrow* regalia is seen heading south at Ais Gill with a *Save The Children Fund Express*, 3 September 1988. RS

Previous pages

165. *Left* Looking like a scene from 1967, Jubilee 4-6-0 *Kolhapur* heads north with the CME on a clear spring day, 31 March 1987.

The snow-decked hills of Langcliffe Scar provide a fine background. RS

166. *Right* The holder of the world speed record for steam traction (126mph) A4 Pacific No 4468 *Mallard* provides a fine spectacle as it approaches Ais Gill summit on the evening of 29 August 1988 with a special train from Eaglescliffe (via Newcastle). RS

169. *Above* On 12 February 1983, Midland Compound 4-4-0 No 1000 (together with Jubilee No 5690 *Leander*) headed the southbound *Cumbrian Mountain Express*.

No 1000 is seen approaching Ais Gill on this very wintry day, a reminder of LMS or even Midland days on the line. RS

167. *Top left* On 28 February 1981, No 4767 (then in LMS black livery) heads south with the CME. The location is Birkett Common. DAVID NIXON

168. *Bottom left* No 4472 pulls away from Ribblehead Viaduct in fine style with the north-bound CME. 29 March 1980. LES NIXON

170. *Above* A broadside view of No 6201 as it heads the northbound
Pennine Pullman near Helwith Bridge on 7 February 1987.
TOM HEAVYSIDE

171. *Top right* LNER Class K1 2-6-0 No 2005 heads north past
Horton-in-Ribblesdale with a NELPG special. 19 March 1983.
Note the beautiful Pullman carriages, painted chocolate and
cream. GAVIN MORRISON

172. *Bottom right* *Evening Star* approaches Dent on 21 April 1984
with a northbound special. Arten Gill viaduct can be dimly seen in
the background. RS

173. *Above* No 46229 *Duchess of Hamilton* leaves Armathwaite
tunnel with the up CME, 9 June 1984. ROBERT LESLIE

174. *Above The Pennine Limited* with No 5305 in charge makes a
vigorous exit as it leaves Appleby, 12 August 1986. RS

175. *Top Sir Lamiel* heads south off Arten Gill viaduct with the
Cumbrian Mountain Pullman, 22 May 1982.
  This viaduct is 220 yards long and has 11 spans. LES NIXON

176. *Above* The northbound CMP hauled by No 5690 *Leander*
heads away from Cotehill, 23 January 1983. LES NIXON

177. 178. *Above and overleaf* Night time at Carlisle Upperby shed, stabling point for S & C locomotives. In the top view, taken on 6 January 1984, we see No 46229 *Duchess of Hamilton*. Midland Compound No 1000 was photographed on the evening of 11 February 1983. RS